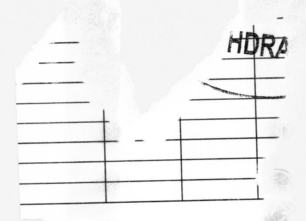

# SCIENCE FAIR PROJECTS

## Forces and Motion

Kelly Milner Halls

Heinemann Library
Chicago, Illinois

Customer Service 888-454-2279
Visit our website at **www.heinemannlibrary.com**

Designed by Kimberly R. Miracle and Fiona MacColl
Illustrations by Cavedweller Studios
Printed in China by WKT Ltd

11 10 09 08 07
10 9 8 7 6 5 4 3 2 1

ISBNs: ISBN-13: 978-1-4034-7910-5(hc)    ISBN-10: 1-4034-7910-0(hc)

**Library of Congress Cataloging-in-Publication Data**
Halls, Kelly Milner, 1957-
  Forces and motion / Kelly Milner Halls.
    p. cm. -- (Science fair projects)
  Includes index.
  ISBN-13: 978-1-4034-7910-5 (hc)
 1.  Science projects--Juvenile literature. 2.  Force and energy--Juvenile literature. 3. Motion--
Juvenile literature.  I. Title.
  Q182.3.H354 2007
  530.078--dc22

**Acknowledgments**
The author and publishers are grateful to the following for permission to reproduce copyright
material: Alamy/OnRequest Images.Inc, **p.16**; Corbis, **pp.** 28 (Duomo), 32 (Lew Robertson), 36
(Macduff Everton), 46; Courtesy of Antibubble.com, **p.** 40; Getty Images **pp.** 6, 8 (Image Bank),
**12, 39, 20** (Photodisc), **15** (Hulton Archive), **24** (Stone); Masterfile/Andrew Douglas, **p.** 4.

Cover photograph reproduced with permission of Masterfile Royalty-free. Background image
from istockphoto.com. Car illustration by istockphoto.com/Brian Sullivan.

**Disclaimer**
All the Internet addresses (URLs) given in this book were valid at the time of going to press.
However, due to the dynamic nature of the Internet, some addresses may have changed, or
sites may have changed or ceased to exist since publication. While the author and publisher
regret any inconvenience this may cause readers, no responsibility for any such changes can be
accepted by either the author or the publisher.

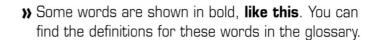

» Some words are shown in bold, **like this**. You can
find the definitions for these words in the glossary.

# Contents

# Science fair Basics

Starting a science fair project can be an exciting challenge. You can test **scientific theory** by developing an appropriate scientific question. Then you can search, using the thoughtful steps of a well-planned experiment, for the answer to that question. It's like a treasure hunt of the mind.

In a way, your mission is to better understand how your world and the things in it work, both together and alone. You may be rewarded with a good grade or an award for your scientific hard work. But no matter what scores your project receives, you'll be a winner. That's because you will know a little bit more about your subject than you did before you started. And you will experience the joy of meeting the challenge.

In this book, we'll look at nine different science fair projects related to forces and motion. We will discover awesome things about the way our planet works.

## Do Your Research

Is there something about the forces and laws of motion of the world that you've always wondered about? Something you don't quite understand but would like to? Then do a little research about the subject. Go to the library and check out books about the subject that interests you.

Use your favorite Internet search engine to find reliable online sources. Museums, universities, scientific journals, newspapers, and magazines are among the best sources for accurate research. Each experiment in this book lists some suggestions for further research.

When doing research you need to make sure your sources are reliable. Ask yourself the following questions about sources, especially those you find online.

## The Experiments

The beginning of each experiment contains a box like this

### Possible Question:

This question is a suggested starting point for your experiment. You will need to adapt the question to reflect your own interests.

### Possible Hypothesis:

Don't worry if your hypothesis doesn't match the one listed here, this is only a suggestion.

### Approximate Cost of Materials:

Discuss this with your parents before beginning work.

### Materials Needed:

Make sure you can easily get all of the materials listed and gather them before beginning work.

### Level of Difficulty:

There are three levels of experiments in this book: Easy, Intermediate, and Hard. The level of difficulty is based on how long the experiment takes and how complicated it is.

1) How old is the source? Is it possible that the information is outdated?

2) Who wrote the source? Is there an identifiable author, and is the author qualified to write about the topic?

3) What is the purpose of the source? The website of a potato chip company is probably not the best place to look for information on healthful diets.

4) Is the information well documented? Can you tell where the author got his or her information?

Some websites allow you to "chat" online with experts. Make sure you discuss this with your parent or teacher before participating. Never give out private information, including your address, online.

Once you know a little more about the subject you want to explore, you'll be ready to ask a science project question and form an intelligent **hypothesis**. A hypothesis is an educated guess about what the results of your experiment will be. Finally, you'll be ready to begin your science fair exploration!

## What Is an Experiment?

When you say you're going to "experiment" you may just mean that you're going to try something out. When a scientist uses that word though, he or she means something else. In a proper experiment you have **variables** and a **control**. A variable is something that changes. The independent variable is the thing you purposely change as part of the experiment. The dependent variable is the change that happens in response to the thing you do. The controlled variables, or control group, are the things you do not change so that you have something to compare your outcomes to. Here's an example: Ten people have headaches. You give 5 people (Group A) asprins. You do not allow 5 people (Group B) to do anything for their headaches. Group A is the independent variable. The effects of the asprins are the dependent variable. Group B is a control group. To make sure the experiment is accurate though, you need to do it several times.

Some of the projects in this book are not proper experiments. They are projects designed to help you learn about a subject. You need to check with your teacher about whether these projects are appropriate for your science fair. Make sure you know all the science fair rules about what kinds of projects and materials are allowed before beginning.

What scientific forces keep this ride on track?

## Your Hypothesis

Once you've decided what question you're going to try to answer, you'll want to make a scientific **prediction** of what you'll discover through your science project.

For example, if you're interested in going fast your question might be "Which goes faster, a skateboard or a scooter?" Remember, a hypothesis is an educated guess about how your experiment will turn out—what results you'll observe. So your hypothesis in response to the above question might be, "Skateboards are faster." The hypothesis is your best guess of how things might turn out when the experiment has been completed. It's also a good way to find out if you can actually complete the steps needed to answer your project question. If your question is, "Can all people be taught to float in water?," it will be impossible to prove your hypothesis, no matter what you make it. This is because you can't test every person in the world. So, be sure the evidence to prove or disprove your hypothesis is actually within reach.

## Research Journal

It is very important to keep careful notes about your project. From start to finish, make entries in your research journal so you won't have to rely on memory when it comes time to create your display. What time did you start your experiment? How long did you work on it each day? What were the variables, or things that changed, about your experimental setting? How did they change and why? What things did you overlook in planning your project? How did you solve the problems, once you discovered them?

These are the kinds of questions you'll answer in your research journal. No detail is too small when it comes to scientific research. You'll find some tips on writing your report and preparing a great display at the back of this book on pages 44–46. Use these and the tips in each project as guides, but don't be afraid to get creative. Make your display, and your project, your own.

# Taking a Tumble

Are you producing **gravity**? Gravity is a universal force, which means it's everywhere and it affects everything. But does gravity have a bigger effect on bigger things? This project will help you understand a little more about gravity and its effects.

## Do Your Research

This project deals with the relationship between an object's size and mass and how gravity affects it. Before you begin your project, do some research to find out more about how mass and size are related to gravity. Once you've done some research, you can tackle this project. Or, you may come up with your own unique project after you've read and learned more about the topic.

Here are some books and websites you could start with in your research:

» Goodstein, Madeline. *Science Fair Success Using Newton's Laws of Motion*. Berkeley Heights, NJ: Enslow, 2002.

» Viegas, Jennifer. *Kinetic and Potential Energy: Understanding Changes within Physical Systems*. New York: Rosen, 2004.

» From Apples to Orbits: The Gravity Story: http//www.library.thinkquest. org/27585

# Project Information

## Possible Question:

Do size and mass affect the speed at which an object falls?

## Possible Hypothesis:

Yes — large, heavy objects will fall faster than small, light objects.

## Level of Difficulty:

Easy

## Approximate Cost of Materials:

$10

## Materials Needed:

» Ten unbreakable objects from around the house. (**Check with your parents for approval of these objects**. Consider an empty plastic food container, a shoe, a book, a stuffed animal, a pencil, a toothbrush, a tennis ball, a soccer ball, etc.)

» A scale to measure the weight of each object

» Tape measure

» A stopwatch

» A ladder

» An adult supervisor to steady the ladder

» An assistant to work the stopwatches

## Steps to Success:

1. Collect ten unbreakable objects of different shapes, sizes, and weights. List each in your journal and record their shapes, sizes, and weights. Before you drop the objects, make some predictions about how they will fall, including which object will fall fastest.

2. Set up your ladder outside and assemble your household items in a pile at the foot of the ladder.

3. Have your assistant ready with the stopwatch. He or she should be ready to activate the stopwatch as soon as you let go of an object, and stop the stopwatch as soon as the object hits the ground. Your assistant will have to watch carefully in order to time things as accurately as possible with the stopwatch.

Continued

**4.** Ask an adult to steady the ladder and to hand you each object as you request it. Climb the ladder.

**5.** Make a note of the exact point from which you are going to drop your object. You should release every object from that same exact point in order for the results to be as accurate as possible. Measure the height of that point, from the ground, and record that information in your research journal.

**Step 6**

**6.** Hold the object in your hand and make sure your assistant is ready with the stopwatch. Drop the object from your release point. Record the object's time in the air, from release to impact, in your research journal.

**7.** Repeat step 6 two more times with the same object. Calculate an average time from the three recorded drops and record that information in your research journal.

**8.** Repeat steps 6 and 7 for each of the other objects.

## Result Summary:

» Did the larger objects fall faster?

» Did the heavier objects fall faster?

» Did your timed results from the first, second, and third drops stay the same for each object?

» Were there major differences in the three times for each object? If so, what might have accounted for that? (Wind? Some other factor?)

## Added Activities to Give Your Project Extra Punch:

» Drop objects that are the same shape, but different weights and sizes — for example, a tennis ball, golf ball, and soccer ball.

» Drop the items from higher and lower points on the ladder and compare the results.

## Display Extras:

» Display some of your dropped items.

# Boing...BoING...BOING

Gravity is a remarkable force of nature. But how does it work when it comes to objects that are alike AND different? This experiment, using three balls of different size and mass but made of the same material, will help you decide if some things feel the pull of the Earth's gravity more than others.

## Do Your Research

This project deals with gravity and whether or not factors such as mass and size have an effect on the strength of gravity's pull. Before you begin your project, do some research to find out more about gravity and how it affects Earth and its natural cycles. Once you've done some research, you can tackle this project. Or, you may come up with your own unique project after you've read and learned more about the topic.

Here are some books and websites you could start with in your research:

» Goodstein, Madeline. *Science Fair Success Using Newton's Laws of Motion.* Berkeley Heights, NJ: Enslow, 2002.

» Exploratorium: Sport/Sciences: That's the Way the Ball Bounces: http://www.exploratorium.edu/sports/ball_bounces/

» PBS Kids ZOOM: Daredevil Ball Jump: http://pbskids.org/zoom/activities/sci/daredevilballjump.html

# Project Information

## Possible Question:

Do different sized balls with different masses bounce the same height?

## Possible Hypothesis:

Smaller balls with less mass will not bounce as high as larger balls with greater mass.

## Level of Difficulty:

Easy

## Approximate Cost of Materials:

$20

## Materials Needed:

**NOTE:** All balls used should be made of the same material.

» Four balls of different sizes made from the same material

» Chalk or washable markers in four different colors

» Ladder

» Masking tape

» Permanent marker

» Tape measure or yard stick

» An assistant

» An adult to hold the ladder

## Steps to Success:

1. Weigh each of the balls and record their weight in your research journal.

2. Set up your ladder in a flat driveway or in an area next to a flat wall.

3. Measure your ladder and make a note of the height in your research journal.

4. **ADULT SUPERVISION REQUIRED** Have an adult hold the ladder steady while you climb to the top of the ladder holding the smallest ball.

5. Ask your assistant to stand three feet away and face the wall, where he or she can see you drop the ball.

6. Ask your assistant to pay close attention to the ball on its first bounce in order to note the spot on the wall where the ball bounces its highest.

Continued

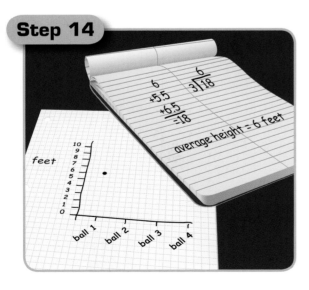

**7.** Drop the smallest ball from the top of your ladder at the height you measured. Be sure to drop the ball from this exact, measured point as your assistant watches. **Do not** put any force behind the drop. Simply let go, so that your results will reflect what the ball does naturally, not what your muscle power can make it do.

**8.** Ask your assistant to stick a piece of masking tape on the wall at the point where the ball bounced the highest. Have your assistant label the piece of masking tape "smallest ball, 1st try."

**9.** Repeat steps 4 through 8 twice more, but having your assistant label the masking tape as "2nd try" and "3rd try" as appropriate.

**10.** Measure the height of each try and record all of the data in your research journal.

**11.** Repeat steps 4 through 10 using the next smallest ball.

**12.** Repeat steps 4 through 10 using the third smallest ball.

**13.** Repeat steps 4 through 10 using the largest ball.

**14.** Calculate the average height that each of the different-sized balls bounced and record those numbers in your research journal.

## Result Summary:

» Did all the balls bounce at the same height, despite their differences in size and mass?

» Did the material the balls were made of affect the results?

» If you repeated the experiment with balls made of a different material, would your results stay the same?

## Added Activities to Give Your Project Extra Punch:

» Repeat the experiment using balls made of a different material.

» Measure, graph, and compare the second, third, and fourth bounces of each ball on each drop, along with the first bounce.

» Try the same experiment using objects of different shape. Does shape have any effect? Why or why not?

## Display Extras:

» Display all of the balls used in your experiment.

» Cut the balls in half and display what they are made of. (**NOTE**: your local home improvement or hardware store may be willing to cut the balls in half for little or no money.)

Sir Issac Newton is often described as discovering gravity. What would he do for a science fair project?

# How DOES the Cookie Crumble?

Do you feel like you're under pressure? Pressure is the force one body uses against another. In this project you'll see how a little pressure can go a long way.

## Do Your Research

This project deals with different scientific forces. Before you begin the project do some research on the different forces in nature. Once you've done some research, you can tackle this project. Or, you may come up with your own unique project after you've read and learned more about the topic.

Here are some books and websites you could start with in your research:

» Viegas, Jennifer. *Kinetic and Potential Energy: Understanding Changes within Physical Systems.* New York: Rosen, 2004.

» Engineering Works: Texas A&M: How does the cookie crumble?: http://engineeringworks.tamu.edu/?p=91

# Project Information

## Possible Question:

How much force does it take to break a fortune cookie?

## Possible Hypothesis:

A fortune cookie will break under 1 pound of pressure.

## Level of Difficulty:

Easy

## Approximate Cost of Materials:

$20

## Materials Needed:

» 3 Fortune cookies (available at many grocery stores or from a Chinese restaurant)
» One sheet of clear, flexible plastic
» Clear tape
» One small piece of cardboard
» 500 pennies
» A food scale
» A ruler
» An assistant

## Steps to Success:

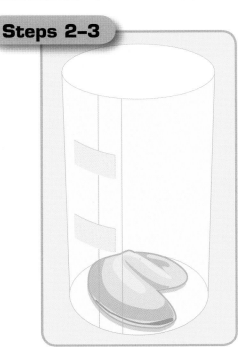

Steps 2–3

1. Measure the precise length of your fortune cookie, from end to end, with a ruler. Record this measurement in your research journal.

2. Roll your sheet of plastic into a tube just wide enough to allow the cookie to sit flat inside it.

3. Measure the **diameter** of the open end of your tube and record that data in your research journal.

4. Use your measurement of the tube's diameter to cut a circle from your piece of cardboard that will fit snugly inside the end of the tube. Put the circle on one end of the tube and tape it in place. This will be the bottom of your tube.

Continued ➔

17

5. Place the tube on a flat surface like a kitchen table or counter.

6. Slip the fortune cookie inside the tube so it rests on the cardboard bottom.

7. Cut a second circle of cardboard just 1/16th of an inch or so less in diameter than the bottom of your tube. It should fit snugly inside the tube, on top of the fortune cookie.

8. Weigh a penny on your scale and make note of its weight in your research journal.

9. Ask your assistant to sit beside the tube so the cookie is at eye level and watch it closely for any sign of breaking.

10. Put a penny in the tube on top of the cardboard circle lying flat over the cookie.

11. Repeat step ten, adding one penny at a time, until some part of the cookie breaks. Keep track of the number of pennies used, and write down the number of pennies it took to cause the first break in your research journal.

12. Keep adding pennies until the cookie is completely crushed under the weight.

13. Take careful notes in your research journal about what part of the cookie breaks and under how many pennies.

14. Multiply the number of pennies that were recorded with each significant break by the weight of a single penny. This will give you the total weight that caused each significant break.

15. Repeat the experiment at least three times to compare your results and calculate an average.

## Result Summary:

» Did the cookie break sooner or later than you expected?

» Do you think the results would have changed if you'd put in more than one penny at a time?

» Do you think other cookies would hold up better?

» What conclusions can you draw about the relationship of mass to the force of gravity?

## Added Activities to Give Your Project Extra Punch:

» Repeat the experiment using two other kinds of cookies and compare your data.

» Repeat the experiment putting ten pennies at a time into the tube instead of one.

» Repeat the experiment putting in 25 pennies at a time, and compare.

» Try the experiment dropping in the pennies from a specific height, rather than placing them inside the tube, and see if it makes a difference.

## Display Extras:

» Display all the materials you used in this experiment to test the durability of a fortune cookie. If possible, set it up so judges and other visitors can repeat your experiment as they walk by your display. If you test the experiment with other cookies, display those as well.

» Display the number of pennies it took to break the cookie on one side of a scale, and one fortune cookie on the other, to demonstrate the difference in weight.

You will make a great discovery

# Paper Caper

When something flies, we sometimes say it "defies gravity," as if it denies gravity the usual power it has over an object. But that's not really true. The act of flying really uses gravity, speed, and lift to make things happen that might seem like magic. People who engineer and plan the construction of airplanes know that what a flying machine is made of can make a big difference in its flying success. This experiment with paper airplanes will help demonstrate that factor.

## Do Your Research

This project deals with flight and how different materials affect an object's ability to fly. Before you begin your project, do some research to find out more about flight, **aerodynamics**, airplanes, and what materials are used to make airplanes. Once you've done some research, you can tackle this project. Or, you may come up with your own unique project after you've read and learned more about the topic.

Here are some books and websites you could start with in your research:

» Stillinger, Doug. *The Klutz Book of Paper Airplanes*. New York: Klutz, 2004.
» Ken Blackburn's Paper Airplanes:  http://www.paperplane.org/

# Project Information

## Possible Question:

Does the kind of paper used change how a paper airplane flies?

## Possible Hypothesis:

No — the airplane will fly the same way, no matter what paper it's made of.

### Level of Difficulty:

Easy

### Approximate Cost of Materials:

$10

## Materials Needed:

» One sheet of notebook paper
» One sheet of typing paper
» One sheet of card stock
» One sheet of newsprint paper
» One sheet of construction paper
» Paper airplane template (this should be easily found in your research materials)
» Tape measure
» An assistant to help with measuring

## Steps to Success:

1. Make sure each of your sheets of paper is the same size. Weigh the paper and record the results.

2. Fold each of your sheets of paper into the same paper airplane. Make sure each of your paper airplanes has the same folds of the same size. You want identical planes, except for the paper used for each one.

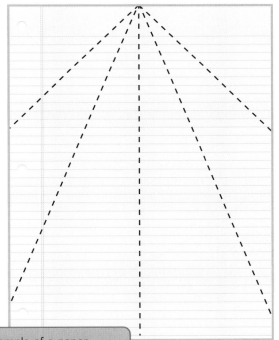

This is an example of a paper airplane template. To make an airplane you would fold the paper along the dotted lines.

Continued

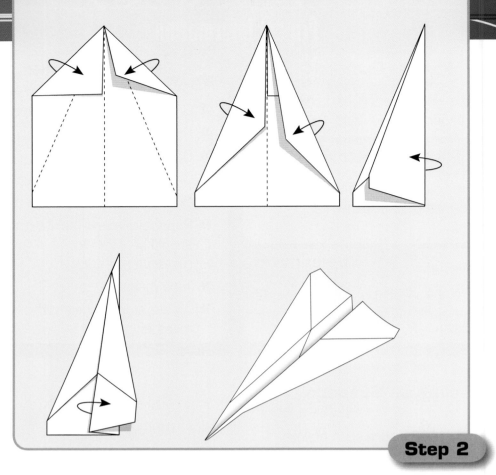

**3.** Mark a spot on the ground outside as your launch pad.

**4.** The goal is to send each airplane soaring using exactly the same motion and speed, in exactly the same direction. You want to try to make each launch identical to the last.

**5.** Launch one of your airplanes. Measure the distance from launch to landing in feet and inches. Record the data in your research journal.

**6.** Repeat step 5 four times with the same airplane and calculate an average distance. Record that data in your research journal.

**7.** Repeat steps 5 and 6 for each of your paper airplanes and record all of the data in your research journal.

**8.** Chart your results, using the average distances for each airplane, to determine if different kinds of paper change how the same paper airplane design flies.

## Result Summary:

» Did each of the airplanes land the same distance from your launch pad?

» Did the heavier paper fly farther?

» Did the light paper fly as far or farther than the heavy paper?

» Were the results what you expected?

» If you were outside, how did weather conditions affect the flight of your airplanes?

» What other factors might have affected the flight of your airplanes?

## Added Activities to Give Your Project Extra Punch:

» Add a paper clip to the nose of each airplane and see if that affects how they fly.

» Do decorated paper airplanes fly better? Decorate and find out. Be sure to add the same decorations to each plane so as not to affect the weight differences of the paper.

» Try the experiment indoors in a gym or other large room.

## Display Extras:

» Display each of your five airplanes, especially if you decided to decorate them. Consider creating a mobile with your airplanes carefully suspended for display, or attach them to your display board.

# free fall for All

In 1483 Leonardo daVinci dreamed of a pyramid shaped parachute made of "gummed" linen. Today's parachutes are not pyramid shaped—and they're usually made of coated nylon. But does that matter? Does the shape of a parachute help keep skydivers safe as they drift toward the ground? This experiment will help you find out.

## Do Your Research

This project deals with gravity and the impact shape has on **wind resistance**. Before you begin your project, do some research to find out more about wind resistance as well as parachutes and other materials that help people fly. Once you've done some research, you can tackle this project. Or, you may come up with your own unique project after you've read and learned more about the topic.

Here are some books and websites you could start with in your research:

» Kind, Lee A. *Airborne: So You Want to be a Jumpmaster*. Fairfax Station, VA: Lee Kind, 2006.

» International Parachuting Commission: http://www.fai.org/parachuting/

» Leonardo da Vinci Museum Exhibit in Italy:
http://www.museoscienza.org/english/leonardo/paracadute.html

# Project Information

## Possible Question:

Does the shape of the parachute affect the landing?

## Possible Hypothesis:

The shape of the parachute will affect its landing.

## Level of Difficulty:

Intermediate

## Approximate Cost of Materials:

$20

## Materials Needed:

» Coated nylon fabric, about two yards. (Available at fabric or crafts stores.)
» Scissors
» String
» Army or other tiny plastic figures approximately 1 to 2 inches tall. One each for as many parachutes as you decide to try. Make sure these figures are identical in size, shape, and weight.
» A ladder
» A stopwatch
» An adult supervisor
» An assistant

## Steps to Success:

**1.** You will need to create parachutes for your figures. You may decide to alter either the shape or the size of the parachute, but make sure to keep one or the other consistent. To the right is one idea for a parachute. You may also find templates online, or create one of your own.

**Step 1**

Continued

**2.** Stand on the ladder with an adult holding the ladder steady. Drop your first figure with its parachute from the ladder and have your assistant time the descent. Repeat three times and determine the average speed of descent.

**ADULT SUPERVISION REQUIRED**

**3.** Repeat for each design and/or size of parachute.

**4.** Record the end results based on your ladder-to-ground observations and chart what you discover. In the first column, list each parachute size and shape. In the second column, record the average speed of descent for each.

## Result Summary:

» Did the shape of the parachutes change the way they hit the ground? How so? Did your results match your predictions?

» Does the shape or size make a difference in how successfully a parachute performs?

» Based on your results, which parachute would you say is the safest? Why?

## Added Activities to Give Your Project Extra Punch:

» Try doubling the "people power" dangling from the parachute.

» Try using larger figures such as dolls or stuffed animals.

## Display Extras:

» Parachutes

» Photos of parachuters

» Your "parachuters"

# Ramp up for Speed

The ramp was one of the earliest tools. It helped people expand their horizons by making life easier—especially when it came to moving heavy objects more quickly. It brought progress within reach. But how much does the angle of a ramp affect acceleration? Try to find out by doing this experiment.

## Do Your Research

This project deals with the forces of acceleration. Before you begin your project, do some research on ramps and acceleration. Once you've done some research, you can tackle this project. Or, you may come up with your own unique project after you've read and learned more about the topic.

Here are some books and websites you could start with in your research:

» Thatcher, Kevin (ed). *Thrasher Presents: How to Build Skateboard Ramps, Halfpipes, Boxes, Bowls, and More.* New York: High Speed Productions, 2004.

» Simple Machines: http://www.sln.fi.edu/qa97/spotlight3/spotlight3.html

» Inclined Planes: http://www.librarythinkquest.org/J002079F/plane.htm

# Project Information

## Possible Question:

How much does the downhill tilt of a ramp affect the speed of a car?

## Possible Hypothesis:

Tilting the ramp more steeply will make cars go faster.

## Level of Difficulty:

Easy

## Approximate Cost of Materials:

$20

## Materials Needed:

» One thin piece of plywood, about 6 inches wide and 3 feet long.

» Bricks or blocks to put under the ramp to increase the angle of incline

» A protractor to measure the height of the ramp and figure the angle of incline

» A toy car

» A stopwatch

» An assistant to time the car's speed of descent

» A tape measure to measure how far the car rolls at each step

## Steps to Success:

1. Put two bricks on the ground and set the plywood on the bricks to make the ramp. Measure the angle of incline and record your results in your research journal.

**Step 1**

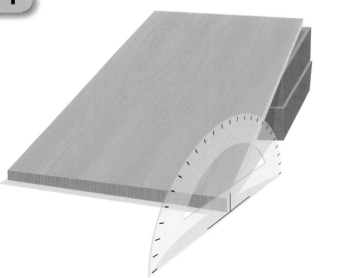

Continued

2. Before rolling the car down the ramp, roll it on the floor from the starting point. Roll it as far as it will go and measure the distance.

3. Hold the toy car at the top of the ramp and let it go. Do not push; just let it roll on its own. Have your assistant start the timer as soon as you let go and time how fast the car rolls down the ramp.

4. Measure the distance the car rolls as well as the time it takes to roll down the ramp.

5. Increase the incline by adding more bricks and repeat steps 3 and 4.

6. Measure the angle of incline at each step and record it in your journal.

## Result Summary:

» Did the ramp incline make the cars go faster? Farther?

» What could you do to change the speed of the cars?

## Added Activities to Give Your Project Extra Punch:

» Try several ramps made of other materials such as tile, metal, and glass.

» Try rolling the car on different surfaces such as carpet, tile floor, etc.

» Try it with cars of different weights and shapes. Compare the figures.

» Visit a skateboard park and study which ramps seem to help skateboarders go the fastest.

## Display Extras:

» Use toy blocks to create miniature versions of your ramp and provide cars so that others can repeat the project.

» Images of different kinds of ramps.

# You Nailed It!

Objects float on water when they displace the water evenly. The object pushes against the surface of the water, but not too hard. If an object got heavier without getting bigger, or got heavier in one place, rather than spreading the weight around evenly, the object might sink. As simple as it sounds, that idea helps people design boats and water transports. Once you do this experiment, you'll see why.

## Do Your Research

This project deals with water and the displacement of water. Before you begin your project do some research to find out more about **buoyancy**, floating, and water. Once you've done your research, you can tackle this project. Or, you may come up with your own unique project after you've read and learned more about the topic.

Here are some books and websites you could start with in your research:

» Cobb, Allan B. *Super Science Projects About Oceans*. New York: Rosen, 2005.

» Nova Online: Buoyancy Basics:
   http://www.pbs.org/wgbh/nova/lasalle/buoybasics.html

» Exploratorium: Buoyancy: http://www.exploratorium.edu/xref/phenomena/buoyancy.html

# Project Information

## Possible Question:

Can nails sink a sponge?

## Possible Hypothesis:

Sponges may normally float in water, but adding too much weight will make them sink.

### Level of Difficulty:

Easy

### Approximate Cost of Materials:

$10

## Materials Needed:

» One 3" x 5" household sponge
» 100 all purpose, one penny nails (available at a hardware store)
» Safety gloves
» One gallon of distilled water and a bucket or dishpan big enough to hold it
» A scale

## Steps to Success:

1. Slip on work or safety gloves to protect your hands from the sharp ends of the nails.

2. Weigh the dry sponge and record your result in your research journal.

3. Place the dry sponge in the water and note how high it sits floating on top of the water.

**Step 3**

Continued →

**Step 6**

4.  Wet your new sponge to make it soft. Wring out the excess water so that the sponge is damp, but not dripping wet. Weigh the damp sponge and record the result.

5.  Place the damp sponge in the water and see how high it sits floating now. Record your impressions in your journal.

6.  Press a nail into each corner of the sponge so that the head of the nail is flush with the sponge and the pointy end is sticking out of the bottom. Try not to squeeze out any water as you press the nail into the sponge. Weigh the sponge now and record the result. Place the sponge in the water and note how it's floating with the added nails.

7.  Wait one minute and note any changes in the level of floatation of the sponge. Take detailed notes in your research journal.

8.  Add four more nails in the middle of each side of the sponge. You want to evenly distribute the weight of the nails in the sponge. Again, weigh the sponge with the added nails and record the result. Then see how high it floats in the water with the added weight.

9.  Keep adding nails four at a time, weighing the sponge each time and then noting how high it floats in the water with the new nails. Keep going until the sponge can no longer float.

## Result Summary:

» Count the nails you've added. Weigh them. How much weight did the damp sponge hold and still float?

» Did the sponge sink once it was full of nails? Why or why not?

» Was the result what you expected?

## Added Activities to Give Your Project Extra Punch:

» Press nails through both sides of the sponge and repeat the experiment.

» Start with a dry sponge and see if there is any difference.

» Try it with a soaking wet sponge.

» Float the sponge with the nails in another liquid and see if the results differ. Try it in soapy water, soda, shampoo, etc.

» Try it in different volumes of water.

» Try it with different types of sponges (round bath sponge, natural sponge, pot scrubber sponge, etc.)

## Display Extras:

» A bowl of nails

» Your sponge before and after it's been filled with nails.

» Pictures of life rafts and other floating objects similar to a sponge to help make the connection between the sponge and real life applications of this knowledge. For example, a raft too full of people is more likely to sink. Caption your picture to be sure you make the point.

# Sinking or floating?

Why do some things float while others sink? It has a lot to do with how **dense,** or tightly compacted, a substance or object is. In other words, if there are air **molecules** evenly distributed in a solid, it is more likely to float. If it's so tightly packed that only very tiny air pockets exist, down it goes. Keep that in mind as you do this experiment with your favorite foods.

## Do Your Research

This project deals with what causes buoyancy, or whether or not an object floats or sinks, and the role density plays in determining that factor. Before you begin your project, do some research to find out more about buoyancy, density, and how they're related, if at all. Once you've done some research, you can tackle this project. Or, you may come up with your own unique project after you've read and learned more about the topic.

Here are some books and websites you could start with in your research:

» Cobb, Allan B. *Super Science Projects About Oceans*. New York: Rosen, 2005.

» Buoyancy Basics: http://www.pbs.org/wgbh/nova/lasalle/buoyancy.html

# Project Information

## Possible Question:

Which foods will float the best?

## Possible Hypothesis:

Light foods like bread will float better than heavier foods like meat.

### Level of Difficulty:

Easy

### Approximate Cost of Materials:

$10

## Materials Needed:

» A 2-quart bowl or pitcher
» Enough water to fill your bowl or pitcher half full
» Eight different food samples
» A watch with a second hand
» Candy or sugar thermometer to test water temperature
» Kitchen scale

## Steps to Success:

1. Fill your bowl or pitcher half full of clean, room-temperature water.

2. Prepare one-ounce samples of eight of your favorite foods. These may be cut into squares, circles, or whatever shape the food is.

3. Drop one of your food samples into the water.

4. Wait three seconds and determine whether the food is sinking or floating, then record the results in your research journal.

### Step 4

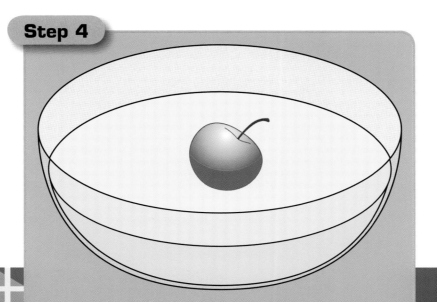

Continued

**5.** Use the watch to time one minute, then look at the food sample again. Is it floating or did it sink? Record the results again in your research journal.

**6.** Repeat steps 3 through 5 with each of the remaining food samples. Change the water each time before you test a new food sample. Use the candy thermometer to test the water temperature with each sample to keep it consistent.

**7.** Chart your final results. Label the first column "Foods" and make a list of each of the food samples. Label the second column "Prediction" and write your prediction of whether the food will sink or float. Next, make two wide columns labeled "One Second" and "One Minute." Under each of these headings, create two more columns, labeled "Floated" and "Sank." In a fifth column, write your notes about what the food samples are made of and what particular characteristics affected their buoyancy, and how this helped you with your predictions.

**Step 7**

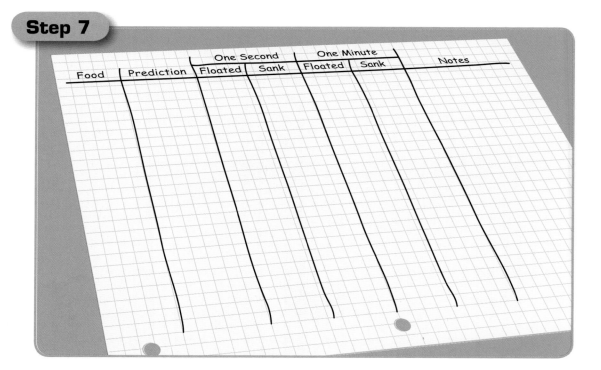

| Food | Prediction | One Second | | One Minute | | Notes |
|------|-----------|------------|------|------------|------|-------|
|      |           | Floated | Sank | Floated | Sank |       |

## Result Summary:

» Which foods floated? Which foods sank?
» Did the result change after one minute had passed?
» Why do you think the food sank or didn't sink?
» Are there any similarities among the foods that floated, if any floated?
» Are there any similarities among the foods that sank, if any sank? Compare and contrast the various foods used.
» What characteristics seemed to most affect the buoyancy of the foods?

These healthful foods will keep you "afloat" during the day, but will they float in water?

## Added Activities to Give Your Project Extra Punch:

» Try the experiment using hot water.
» Try the experiment using ice water.
» Try leaving the foods in the water for longer periods of time.
» Try using cooking oil instead of water and comparing the difference between cooking oil and water.
» Try timing the different food samples and noting how many seconds pass before they actually do sink, if they sink.

## Display Extras:

» Samples of your foods, before and after being placed in the water. You may want to store your food samples in plastic baggies for easy identification and display.
» Before and after photos of your food samples. (Photos are always less of a mess with an experiment like this.)

# Bubble, Bubble

If air pockets cause some objects to float, it make sense that bubbles, which are air pockets we can see, also float. But did you know there are **antibubbles** — air pockets you can see underwater? If you patiently conduct this experiment, you'll soon believe.

## Do Your Research

This project deals with buoyancy, the conditions needed to create antibubbles, and the observed properties of antibubbles. Before you begin your project, do some research to find out more about buoyancy and antibubbles. Once you've done some research, you can tackle this project. Or, you may come up with your own unique project after you've read and learned more about the topic.

Here are some books and websites you could start with in your research:

» Stein, David. *How to Make Monstrous, Huge, Unbelievably Big Bubbles.* Palo Alto, CA: Klutz Press, 2005.

» Antibubble.org: http://www.antibubble.org/

# Project Information

## Possible Question:

How are antibubbles created?

## Possible Hypothesis:

Antibubbles are created when liquid is inside liquid.

| Level of Difficulty: | Approximate Cost of Materials: |
|---|---|
| Hard | $10 |

## Materials Needed:

» 1 large pitcher (that will hold at least 20 ounces)

» 1 large, clear, 12-ounce drinking glass

» 1 wide, flat bowl in which you'll be able to set the drinking glass

» 1 small 4-ounce cup or container

» A baby nasal bulb syringe (in the pharmacy with baby supplies)

» A paperclip

» Clear dish soap (avoid the milky ones)

» Ordinary table salt

» A tablespoon measuring spoon

» Camera

## Steps to Success:

1. In your large pitcher, mix 16 ounces of tap water with 2 tablespoons of dish soap and 2 pinches of salt. Don't let it get foamy (You're going for antibubbles, not bubbles!). Leave it to sit overnight so the solution stabilizes.

2. Set the clear drinking glass inside the wide, flat bowl.

3. Fill the 12-ounce drinking glass to the brim with the soapy solution, saving 4 ounces in a cup on the side. **CAUTION**: Be careful when handling a glass container and soapy water at the same time. The soapy water can make the glass very slippery.

4. Allow the mixture to sit for 30 minutes to clear any foam.

Continued

**5.** Unbend the paperclip and wrap it around the tip of the bulb syringe with a "tail" sticking out beyond the squirting tip.

**6.** Fill the bulb syringe with the same soapy mixture by squeezing the bulb to push the air out, then dipping the tip in the soapy water, releasing the bulb, and allowing the water to fill it up.

**7.** Hold the syringe just above the surface of the water in the glass, with the wire (end of what was the paperclip) touching the water's surface.

**8.** Gently squirt the soapy water from the syringe into the glass, with the wire continuing to touch the water's surface in order to **ground** your experiment (otherwise static electricity can pop your antibubbles before they appear). It may take some practice to create an antibubble. Start by squirting the water from the bulb into the glass gently, then more and more strongly until you see antibubbles forming. The antibubbles will look like regular bubbles, but with an extra layer inside. Remember from your research that antibubbles are liquid surrounded by a thin layer of air, surrounded by liquid.

**9.** Take pictures of your antibubbles. They are very fragile and pop easily, so have your camera ready. If you have trouble forming antibubbles that last long enough, you may want to find an assistant for taking pictures.

## Result Summary:

» Were you able to create your own antibubbles? If so, what method worked best?

» What are antibubbles and what forces make them possible?

» Why do you think soapy water makes it easier to create antibubbles?

» What happens when antibubbles pop?

» What would you change if you were to try this project again?

## Added Activities to Give Your Project Extra Punch:

» Add more salt to the solution you inject into the glass to make heavier antibubbles that sink to the bottom of the bowl.

» Add food coloring to the solution you inject to create colored antibubbles.

» Add a layer of honey to the bottom of the water glass so that the heavier antibubbles will not pop as quickly when they settle at the bottom.

## Display Extras:

» Pictures of antibubbles other people have made.

» Use the same solution, but with food coloring, and create colored antibubbles to draw attention to your display as you wait for judges. Other people may want to try it as well if they see you creating them right there. Check the rules of your science fair first to make sure this is okay.

# The Competition

Learning is it's own reward, but winning the science fair is pretty fun, too. Here are some things to keep in mind if you want to do well in competition:

1) Creativity counts. Do not simply copy an experiment from this or any other book. You need to change the experiment so that it is uniquely your own.

2) You will need to be able to explain your project to the judges. Being able to talk intelligently about your work will help reassure the judges that you learned something, and did the work yourself. You may have to repeat the same information to different judges, so make sure you've practiced it ahead of time. You will also need to be able to answer the judge's questions about your methods and results.

3) You will need to present your materials in an appealing manner. Discuss with your teacher whether or not it is acceptable to have someone help you with artistic flourishes to your display.

## Keep these guidelines in mind for your display:

» **Type and print:** Display the project title, the question, the hypothesis, and the collected data in clean, neatly crafted paper printouts that you can mount on a sturdy poster display.

» **Visibility:** Be sure you print your title and headings in large type and in energetic colors. If your project is about the Sun, maybe you'll use bright reds, oranges, and yellows to bring your letters to life. If your project is about plant life, maybe you'll use greens and browns to capture an earthy mood. You want your project to be easily visible in a crowd of other projects.

» **Standing display:** Be sure your display can stand on its own. Office supply stores have thick single-, double-, and triple-section display boards available in several sizes and colors that will work nicely as the canvas for your science fair masterpiece. Mount your core data — your discoveries — on this display, along with photos and other relevant materials (charts, resource articles, interviews, etc.).

» **Dress neatly and comfortably for the fair.** You may be standing on your feet for a long time.

4) The final report is an important part of your project. Make sure the following things are in your final report:

» **A title page:** the first page of your report, with your name and the name of your project (similar to page 1 of this book)

» **A table of contents:** what's included in your report (similar to page 3 of this book)

» **Research:** the research you did that led you to choose this topic and help you to formulate your question

» **Your project question:** what you tested

» **Your hypothesis:** your prediction of how your experiment would answer the question

» **Materials:** the things you used to conduct your experiment

» **Methods:** the steps you took to perform your experiment

» **Observations:** some of the things you recorded in your research journal

» **Conclusion:** how closely your hypothesis lined up with the results

» **Bibliography:** books, articles, and other resources you used in researching and preparing your project. Discuss with your teacher the appropriate way to list your sources.

» **Acknowledgments:** recognition of those who helped you to prepare and work on your project

# Prepare to Be Judged

Each science fair is different but you will probably be assigned points based on the categories below. Make sure to talk to your teacher about how your specific science fair will be judged. Ask yourself the questions in each category to see if you've done the best possible job.

## Your objectives
» Did you present original, creative ideas?
» Did you state the problem or question clearly?
» Did you define the variables and use controls?
» Did you relate your research to the problem or question?

## Your skills
» Do you understand your results?
» Did you do your own work? It's OK for an adult to help you for safety reasons, but not to do the work for you. If you cannot explain the experiment, the equipment, and the steps you took, the judges may not believe you did your own work.

## Data collection and interpretation
» Did you keep a research journal?
» Was your experiment planned correctly to collect what you needed?
» Did you correctly interpret your results?
» Could someone else repeat the experiment?
» Are your conclusions based only on the results of your experiment?

## Presentation
» Is your display attractive and complete?
» Do you have a complete report?
» Did you use reliable sources and document them correctly?
» Can you answer questions about your work?

# Glossary

**aerodynamics** study of how air moves

**antibubble** opposite of a bubble, which is a sphere of air surrounded by a thin film of water. An antibubble is a droplet of water surrounded by a thin film of air.

**buoyancy** ability to float

**control** something that is left unchanged in order to compare results against it

**data** factual information

**dense/density** amount of something in a specific area

**diameter** distance through the center of an object from one side to the other

**gravity** attraction of bodies to the center of the Earth

**ground** connect electrically with the ground

**hypothesis** supposition or educated guess based on information at hand

**molecule** smallest portion of a substance

**prediction** to say in advance what you think will happen, based on scientific study

**scientific theory** belief based on tested evidence and facts

**variable** something that could change; is not set or fixed

**wind resistance** pull on an object as it moves through the air

# Index